PENGUIN

The Speculations o

Majella Kelly is an award-winning Irish writer whose appeared in the *Irish Times*, *Poetry Ireland Review*, *Ambit*, *Rialto*, *Best New British and Irish Poets 2017* and *Aesthetica*'s *Creative Writing Annual*. In 2020, her debut pamphlet, *Hush*, was published by Ignition Press, and ten of these poems appeared in the University of Leeds/Carcanet *Brotherton Prize Anthology*. She won the Ambit Poetry Prize in 2018 and the Strokestown International Poetry Prize in 2019, and has been shortlisted for several other awards, including the Gregory O'Donoghue International Poetry Prize, the *Irish Times* Hennessy Literary Award, the Resurgence Eco Poetry Prize (now the Gingko Prize) and the Listowel Poetry Collection Award. She holds a master's in Creative Writing from the University of Oxford.

MAJELLA KELLY

The Speculations of Country People

PENGUIN BOOKS

PENGUIN BOOKS

UK | USA | Canada | Ireland | Australia
India | New Zealand | South Africa

Penguin Books is part of the Penguin Random House group of companies
whose addresses can be found at global.penguinrandomhouse.com

First published 2023
001

Set in 10/13.75pt Warnock Pro
Typeset by Jouve (UK), Milton Keynes
Printed and bound in Great Britain by Clays Ltd, Elcograf S.p.A.

The authorized representative in the EEA is Penguin Random House Ireland,
Morrison Chambers, 32 Nassau Street, Dublin D02 YH68

A CIP catalogue record for this book is available from the British Library

ISBN: 978–1–802–06172–7

www.greenpenguin.co.uk

Penguin Random House is committed to a
sustainable future for our business, our readers
and our planet. This book is made from Forest
Stewardship Council® certified paper.

To Mary Anne and Walter, my Mam and Dad

What it takes, on this planet,
to make love to each other in peace
— Pablo Neruda

Shame requires
the eyes of others
unlike guilt

— Anne Carson

CONTENTS

I. SONGS OF LONGING

I Am From

I am from Kelly, Henebry, Burke, Scully.
Hill. Mulligan. Cullinane . . .

I am from Laurence and Bridget.
From thatch craft and rosary beads.
His brown eyes. Her aversion to moths.

Irish-from-elsewhere. So they say. Armada flotsam.
Swarthy and afraid. Ship's captain or galley slave –
either way, dodging execution, high above the Glen men.
Sea legs turn sure-footed as a Shepherd.

Hush, hush. Only the gush of mountain streams
to witness his romanic tongue
which over time married itself to those Celtic notes
that floated up from Moonaboola, Glencushabinna and Round Hill.
Even as far as Deerpark, where one day his seed would be blown,
by then his name forgotten.

Today, you will find me near the fairy fort
on a level place, east of the gates. Togher,
safe passage through the wetlands.

But look not out over the quagmire.
Be not bewitched by the foolish fire of the hinkypunk,
where Pop played, in nineteen hundred and ten,
after the eviction, with his siblings.

Julia, Nora, Margaret. Mamie, Ellie, Delia. John. Patrick. William.

Six girls. Three boys. Nine lives. Let's hold hands . . . and sing.
A ring-a-ring-a-rosie. Quick! A tissue! Daddy's got pneumonia.
Honora is a widow.

I am from Kathleen and Willie-Joe.
From sewing machines and pipe tobacco.
Whitewash. Milk churns balanced on a bicycle.

I am from the land, on my hands and knees.
There, in the beet field, thinning.
Out, in the stony field, picking.
Down, in the bog, footing.
Abroad, in the hay field, balanced on the bales stacked in the trailer.

Over in Ardnamoher, in eighteen sixty-six.
Daddahind sits by the window, cross-legged, on a table.

Auntie Lil remembers crying with her sister
when they found out he was dying.
She was only nine; older now than he was at the time.
Edmond Hill could cut as well as sew –
which was important, you know.

In the mirror, I can see him, under my skin, in tailor pose – sewing –
from where I sit on my yoga mat, just breathing.

Sex

A yellow hammock bowed
    between two willows.
        A trout swims upriver.

White truffles. Fruiting
    bodies, under cover.
        Whiskey, musk, chocolate.

An unexpected windfall
    of plums. Long wet grass.
        Ripe fox. Purple tongues.

Cortège to Omey Island as Umbilical Cord

Omey, you have been a receptacle for the dead
for as long as anyone can remember,
but when a vein of cars issues from the churchyard
on the mainland across the strand
at low tide, I consider you more womb
than tomb; your graveyard a belly-button
tethered to the funeral cortège, your
coastline foetal, its crown-rump length of pink
quartz equal to this mile-long cord of nutrient-rich
bodies coming back to be buried where they were born,
in a place so heavy with descendants
its tidal waters keep breaking, pushing bones back up
from the sand swaddled in dandelions,
in wild pansy and low-growing thyme.

Funeral

i.m. Jimmy & Angela

What I remember of the day is white.
White as the keening of the windscreen

    wipers under the blizzard at Seaham.
    White as the taste of a snowflake fallen

        through salty air. White as teardrops
        of wave-soothed sea-glass. White as a plume

            of his bones made ash, fluent on the cold
            air as a gannet, which is the same colour

        as a white flag. White as the noise the telly
        makes at night when she falls asleep again

    in his chair. White as the dream she still has
    of the Limerick lace she sewed into the dress

she wore on their wedding day. White as the gaps
in his mind her name had long since fallen through.

Portrait of the City with Mastectomy

The city is a woman and I almost can't look.
Someone has ripped off her red and white dress
which was the gigantic FOR SALE sign, taken a scalpel
to her skin which was the façade of the Capitol Cinema
on Grand Parade, cleaved the flesh on the wall
of her chest which is red bricks and grey mortar,
clamped a rib-spreader between her shoulders
which are Tom Murphy's Dress Hire and a late night
pharmacy, in order to hold back organs and tissue
which are dumper trucks, piles of rubble and a team
of men in hard hats and high-visibility vests.
Nobody should be able to see right through
the lungs of the city like that, as if through the gaping
back side of a surgical gown, as far as Patrick Street,
whose buildings are a row of vertebrae which boats
once navigated and where pedestrians now bustle
as if nothing remarkable has happened.
Human eyes weren't meant to probe the dark
alveoli of abandoned rooms in the Oyster Tavern
from here, inspect the artery of Market Lane
or witness the scaffolding and steel girders holding up
the old Meat Market like surgical instruments.
Black plastic bandages flap in the wind, amplifying
the persistent coughing of pneumatic drills,
and all of a sudden there's Auntie Anne on a red
velour seat hovering in a ghostly confetti of ticket stubs.
Two shillings and sixpence she paid to sit up there
in the balcony. Now the yellow scoop of a digger
is my mother's hand manoeuvring a final Silk Cut
Purple to her lips, while the city holds the blue arm
of a crane across her breasts to hide the scars.

Clipping a Cockatiel's Wings (For Dummies)

Start by clipping the two outermost flight feathers.
A week later, clip the next two. Continue this schedule
until the ten primary feathers have been trimmed.
If she is likely to get out through an open window
she may need a more severe clip; the same if she is bossy,
since being more dependent on you will curb her attitude.
Don't risk taking her outside on your shoulder. Train her
to use a leash or a harness; you'd be surprised how well
a clipped cockatiel can get about. Also, don't clip blood
feathers as it will be painful and cause your bird to bleed.
Blood feathers siphon blood. Sometimes, the only way
to stop the flow is to pull out that shaft with a quick,
firm movement while supporting her wing bones.
She will gradually have lost the ability to fly but will still
need some wing exercise, so take some time every day
to hold her feet and encourage her to flap – chances are
she'll develop strong chest muscles and be well able
to hop around her cage. Be sure to do a symmetrical job,
however: it looks better, and she'll be more balanced.
The last thing you want to do is make her clumsy.

She needs to know who's boss:
it's your house, after all.
To know her whereabouts,
ensure she has no money,
get her email password,
take away her phone.
Bruise, don't break,
just to deter; no more.
Although it's not a crime,
the kids might notice.
If she tries to tell anyone,
say she hit into the door:
Tell her, if she loves you,
to keep her beak shut,
that she was asking for it.
Have the last word.
You alone understand,
it's for her own good.
See her lopsided mother?
She could never leave her cage.

Cold Case

It was a sheltered place and considered safe for swimming. Three miles outside the town, at night the spot was popular with courting couples and, in the mornings, joggers.

That day, the water was clear and the sand almost white. A man was going for a run along the shoreline inhaling the gentle wetness of seashells, samphire, brassica.

Then a certain animal funkiness. It was just a doll, he told himself. A pink doll with black hair. Or maybe it was a bird? A fledgling that had been terrified how soon it was for its flimsy yet exquisite wings to support it.

But there were no trees, no nest for it to slip from, only a grey fertilizer bag lying limp beside it. The man couldn't see its face, the way its little beak was jammed into a space between two rocks, but he blessed himself anyway.

*

It was the undertaker christened him John. And it was the undertaker's daughter who gathered her friends in their school uniforms to escort the unloved flesh and bones of him into the cemetery. *Be Not Afraid* they sang, the sound as sweet that morning as any dawn chorus.

*

Though nobody ever left flowers on the grave, the plain wooden cross went unmolested for many years. But when the new headstone, flecked with feathers of gold, was only five days old, somebody waited in the shadows of the ditches to smash it to pieces with a sledgehammer, black granite fragments of the words *I forgive* left scattered in the grass.

Nobody in the locality ever admitted to hearing the headstone cry out in the night, even though twenty-eight times it was punctured in the frenzy, and four of those to its heart.

Saint v Goddess

You asked me why I slipped something silver
into my schoolbag on the last day of winter.
I'd read, you see, how the goddess Brigid
was a silversmith, how she brought a whistle
of silver with her, so wherever she went
she'd never feel alone: its call was enough
to summon her friends at a run. And since this
was the eve of her feast day, I said I'd slip something
silver into my schoolbag. You asked why I left
school at lunchtime and went to the grotto alone.
Well, I didn't go there to pray. I went to lie down
in the grass. And because I clenched the whistle
hard between my teeth and I blew and blew
like a goddess would, I didn't feel alone,
though it was cold and wet, and nobody came.
Only the wind whistled through the oak tree.

Listen, loveen, the oak said: they kept our beloved
Brigid's feast day, but then they built the churches,
shut the doors, and called the goddess *Saint*.
Saint Brigid preached virginity. She never felt
her body's pleasure at another's touch,
nor ever felt that rush-onto-the-battlefield loss –
not as the goddess Brigid felt it, the day that
she invented keening. There are no druids, either,
the rowan tree whispered: only priests
who'll tell you it was your *immaturity* did this,
not any lack of Christian charity. And definitely
no priestesses left, the old hare said as she nuzzled

my neck, forgetting herself. Sister Immaculata
will say she never knew – the whole town, too.
Rest now. I'll swaddle him in your school coat
once I've cut the cord with your silver scissors.

How to Measure the Happiness of a Lake

You'd be wrong if you think you can measure Lough Corrib's happiness by the proliferation of its mayfly hatch. Nor can it be measured by the number of fish it allows you to catch; that would also be an unreliable measurement of the lake's happiness. So, if you don't manage to catch a single trout or salmon this year, you shouldn't take it personally, that's just the way of the lake. It's not selfishness on the lake's behalf, more like a rationing of its future happiness. And anyway, the lake doesn't understand the word *begrudgery*. The lake isn't like some Irish people who dislike those with 'notions'. It's true that famous people are left to themselves when they are out on the lake, but that's not because the lake thinks they are no better than the rest of us. The lake doesn't go around nudging other lakes and muttering: *He's awful fond of himself, isn't he,* if someone has a bigger engine on his boat than anyone else. Or: *Who does she think she is?* if she's decked out in designer fishing gear. Or: *A pity about you,* when another fish has slipped your hook. That's because a lake doesn't assume that there's only so much happiness to go around and that it's not getting enough of it.

Of course, it isn't exactly clear what qualifies as happiness, the way it isn't exactly clear what a game fish is. If a game fish is classified by its eating value, then perhaps sturgeon and herring should be game too, but not everyone agrees. If classified according to fighting qualities then pike could be a worthy antagonist, because on suitable tackle some say it can give the same performance as salmon. Yet those living close to the lake will strongly disagree.

And another thing. It's impossible to measure a lake's happiness from the shore. You must borrow a fishing rod and a small wooden boat and row out into the middle of the lake in the early morning when the islands are golden and crafty like pagans. (Be sure to bring a flask of tea and some sandwiches.) Morning is better, when the gulls are actively hunting. It's hard to be out on the lake after the gulls are done. There's something about them, flying low, going home, having had what there is to be had.

However many strokes of the oars it takes, that is the radius of the lake's happiness, an ache-in-the-biceps type of happiness; and one that's exponential. Let the boat drift here a while and think about all the oars that have stroked these waters over the centuries. Not only those of the fisherman, but those of the druid and the holy recluse; of the bard, the rush-gatherer, and the Nordic warrior. That's the depth of the lake's happiness. It's generational and therefore deeper than any scientific measurement of depth. And so it is fathomless.

Trail your fingers from the boat. This is hoary water, the kind that has come back to live in this lake more than once and remembers every kindness, like an old dog that rolls over on its belly when you enter a room. As you do this, you should recite as many names as you can remember of its one thousand three hundred and twenty-seven islands back to it. That never fails to tickle the lake. So, for example:

Inchagoill, Inchiquin, Inismacatreer,
Carbry & Showery Island,
Brointín, Bertrasaggart, Bertrahippeen,
Earcán Mór & Earcán Beag,
Mucladh & Malachy,
Whiskey Island & Wiltyrogue,
Illaunawullagh, Illaunafinnoge, Illaunabuckedia,
Rabbit, Otter, & Small Goat Island.

Lastly. Put your hook through a daddy-longlegs, at the thick part where the legs meet the body, and let the wind take your line out over the water. Dapping with a daddy-longlegs is a dangly sort of happiness, the kind you might find in a hammock over wild-flowers on a sunny day. But it's tricky to measure. So just dap until it starts to rain. Then count the raindrops piercing the skin of the lake like the tiny spears of fairy folk. See how it looks as if hundreds of thousands of eyes are opening and closing and looking right through you? Now. Keep counting, until you have forgotten all about yourself.

Sonnet for the Glass Blower

Look, Ma, mermaid tears! he says, hands over
-flowing with seafoam, cobalt and honey
-amber glass fragments, sharp edges wave
-mended but new skins etched with tiny 'c's
like echoes of a shipwreck's quiet sobbing.
This one from Pirates' Cave is my favourite.
He lifts it to the sun to show me why.
The bubble inside reminds me of searching
a foetal scan for a heartbeat. A bottle
of milk of magnesia once, it's been holding
the glass-blower's breath in its belly since
blown into life. I thumb its smooth curve
the way you would a bottom lip, the dimple
of air blue and still in its small glass womb.

II. SONGEENS FOR THE HOME BABIES

In 2013 Catherine Corless wrote an article about the Tuam Mother and Baby Home for the local historical society's journal. Her research led to the discovery of the deaths of 796 children in The Home between 1925 and 1961 and, significantly, the absence of any burial records for them. In 2017, after intense media pressure, the Irish government eventually initiated a Commission of Investigation and acknowledged the presence of a mass grave in a disused sewage system on the site of the former Home. Catherine, along with survivors and relatives, campaigned for a full forensic examination of the site and for the children's remains to be given a respectful burial. In February 2022, an Institutional Burials Bill was signed into law so that excavation of the site could take place. It is hoped that DNA-based identification might reunite some families with the remains of their loved ones. Work on the site has yet to begin.

If you come here you'll find no mass grave, no evidence that children were ever so buried, and a local police force casting their eyes to heaven and saying, 'Yeah, a few bones were found – but this was an area where famine victims were buried. So?'

— The Bon Secours religious order, via a PR consultant,
in response to juvenile human remains
at Tuam's former Mother and Baby Home

The Seventh Acre

A memorial garden squats on a small parcel
of land behind a row of houses like a Síle
-na-Gig hunkered and holding her genitals
open like two halves of an apple. A ruminant
garden, her belly's distended by numerous
stomachs. If you come here you'll find her
chewing her cud, coughing up a mandible
perhaps, or an ankle, spitting out tiny pips
of spinal column. Somebody saw a small boy
once running across her shorn scalp rattling
a skull on a stick. For this is the seventh acre,
the acre that ate babies, but only the ones
whose mothers were sinners, ones it was right
to leave nightly rocking themselves to sleep.

In Bosch's 'Garden of Earthly Delights'

I am drawn to the small figure of a man
approached by a pig wearing a nun's veil.
I think of my father as a boy, how he
was made to stop on his way to school
in Tuam by the sisters of the Bon Secours.
Obediently he'd wait while the big doors
in The Home's high perimeter wall dilated
just enough for the *babies* to issue swiftly
two-by-two in a mad clatter of hobnail boots.
A snake of shorn heads, distended bellies
and snotty noses would make its way
across Dublin Road. *Be good*, he was told,
or you'll be put in with the Home Babies.

How essential it was to Christianity,
I think then, to paint an unsettling picture
of a place we must live in fear of,
where the fallen face the consequences
of sensual pleasure, a place where the tree
-man lives, his torso a broken eggshell,
whose cavity is a tavern for naked men.
A place of grotesqueries whose diabolical
prince sits on a potty-throne excreting
people, a cauldron on his head. Cities
were burning, for all my father knew, rivers
could be freezing and animals feeding
on human flesh behind those grey high walls.

There Go I

Everyone turned to stare when the hare turned
up at the back of the church like a twitching
bride ready to walk up the aisle. Of course
a hare can't walk exactly, for, no matter
how slowly she moves among the mangel
-wurzels or the oilseed rape, she looks ungainly.
A hare has no interest in marriage, either,
since she likes to be promiscuous, doesn't
care that some would call her leverets *bastards*
by different fathers. And regardless of
how many times her nest gets trodden on,
she'd never call it *broken*. Nor does she feel
she's failed at life. On the contrary, like the day
you were born, furred, your eyes wide open.

Crab-apple

This particular tree is legitimate.
Deliberately grown, it's not one of those
misbegotten lot that grew true from a pip
dropped by a waxwing or a blackbird
in a forest or a hedgerow. In autumn
its harvest was precious, each crab-apple
fondly thumbed like a bead of a rosary,
a jewel treasured for pies and jellies.

But the garden where it was originally
planted got neglected. Next to an ancient
septic tank, this once noble, now ruffian,
of the woods withered to skin and bone,
leaves puckered, twigs curled into shepherds'
crooks. There was something not quite clean
about it, cankers on its bark oozing
a cloudy liquid in cold damp weather

like the snot-filled noses of children
with no one to care for them. Then one year
the crop was left to rot in the grass.
The loss of the sweet pink jam on the tongues
of the nuns come winter was briefly grieved
but by and by the gravity of the fall of one
small and sour fruit was comparable
to one more baby born out of wedlock.

Voice

To go into The Home was to be given
your voice on a spoon and told: swallow it.
When they shaved our heads, our voices wilted
on our tongues like cut nettles in empty cups.
When they took our names away, the tiny
venomous hairs of shame bored untold holes
in our throats. When they insisted on silence
on the birthing table, just to remind
us we had sinned, the itchy hives of guilt
distended, red and angry, in our bellies.

And when she said: *the child of your sin is dead,*
my heart was an extinguished fireplace.
But when I opened my mouth to cry out,
I spoke only in a thin grey wisp of smoke.

Dandelions

I have come to listen for the lost voices of the children. I know they are here. They are here absolutely. I lie on a blanket of dandelions, my ear to the garden's secret crypt beneath. The only sound is a bicker of bones as rats shift in its pitch-black; the brittle sound of a fleshless kind of darkness. *Pissenlit*. Bitter weed or pretty flower? All day their smiling faces follow the sun as if to ask at any moment: are you our mother? The dandelions are a chalice veil. No typical chalice this. Not buried as treasure. Not gilded or jewel-encrusted. Not curved, either, like the crook of an arm where a baby's head might rest, but angular like a *cul-de-sac* of hidden grief. Beside me lies a monstrance. The glass case at its centre where the communion host goes is perfect for the exposition of a dandelion head. A sunburst within a sunburst. I am a sinner, not because I've stolen the monstrance from the nearby cathedral, but due to the extra-marital sex I engage in for my pleasure and the pleasure of my lover. Sinners are forbidden to eat the Body of Christ, but I suck on it anyway. Then I let a yellow petal dissolve slowly on my tongue. Its bitterness is a truth that's hard to swallow. But things of melancholic hue can be used against melancholy, sour against sour. While in the cathedral I swung a thurible from my left hand. That made me a thurifer. What, then, if I hold this monstrance in both hands heavenward: am I a monster? *Blessèd be the dandelions*, I say out loud. *Let the dandelions come to me, do not hinder them.* It's then they start to tremble and call me by my name, and when I recognize their voices the spell is broken. Patrick, Mary, Peter, Julia, Michael, Sheila, Philomena, Female Roche, Male O'Brien, Baby Forde, Baby Kelly. Little flames, they begin to glow like a small town at dusk, all its curtains undrawn.

Virginia Creeper

talking to a remnant of the boundary wall

Shade makes me aggressive. I twist my hair.
I stare at my hands. Don't say *oppressor*.
I'm afraid of the dark. When I grip the throats
of those weaker it's not that I want to
choke them. I need to reach your pretty neck
-lace of broken glass. I just cut myself
so you'll love me. Stop saying I'm clingy.
It's not my fault all my thoughts are flawed.
My bootless shoots rooted where they fell
and I fasten myself to you for good reason.
You could be ripped from me while I'm sleeping!
Please. Be my mother. I know my little
green flowers aren't worthy and these blue-black
berries toxic, but in autumn I'll make
you proud. Watch me set my every leaf ablaze.

Skull in the Sand

One morning the tide drops a skull at my feet.
A handful of small shells roly-poly

from its nose-holes, strands of seaweed fan
about its empty head and the sea foams

from its open mouth like a muffled conversation
about drowning. Instead of reburying it

I place it in the crook of some rocks
so the cliffs might cradle it and the sea sing

it ancient songs of wild salmon searching
for the scent of their home river.

At first the wind wallops through the eye
-sockets with all its hollow impossible thoughts.

But soon the sky is heady with the smell
of wild mint and heather, not to mention

the small-talk of a wren. Before long it is jammers
with twigs and moss and feathers

and the only thing on its mind by spring
are five perfect white eggs with red speckles.

Over-painting

In the same way that Rudolph II
had the babies in Bruegel's *Massacre
of the Innocents* over-painted, so men
from Galway County Council were sent
with spades and grass seeds to lay a lawn
over the septic tank where juvenile
human remains were known to be found.

In the same way the nuns kept insisting
that no children were ever so buried.

In the painting a woman weeps over
an array of cheese and charcuterie,
which creates a scene arguably more
resonant of calculated evil;
the absence of blood and gore more eerie
and still than the heinous original.

The Old Hare

A hare limps slowly through the deep narrow rooms under the Memorial Garden muttering to herself. She is old and worn out. Her top lip is split and her teeth protrude. *All the goddesses are gone,* she spits. *Banished with the snakes and replaced with saints. Saints! What use are saints down here? And what bloody good were they up there? Saint Gerard Majella, my arse!* The roots of the crab-apple stretch to caress her rough grey pelt. *Be patient,* they tell her, *a new goddess will come, you'll see.*

What did they ever see in Christianity? the old hare continues. *The pagans never named any child 'bastard'. And was it Christian to toss their bodies in an old septic tank such as this like an empty chicken carcass, stripped and boiled up for soup?* Hares are skittish in captivity. Rabbits are the sociable ones, the ones more likely to let a human cradle them. And yet the old hare stays.

There's a soft thud like a just-shot pheasant, and she sits with her ears back listening to the hushed voices above her as they slither along the shadow of the high wall, which bears so lightly its crown of broken glass:

Oh, sister, I feel sorry for the baby. It's still a human being, isn't it?

That child's mother was not *married. Understand this, we are in charge of the soul here.*

The old hare rises again. She catches moonlight by cotton corners that peep through the cracked concrete slab and tucks it under a cold white chin. *Always remember your mother loved you very much,* she reassures the still little bundle, *and that she would've taken you with her if she could.*

At dawn a vigil of robins hover over the makeshift crypt, plucking out their own breast feathers so its darkness be silken and tinged with pink. Then ravens, in their black shawls, process solemnly through the brambles bearing forget-me-nots.

Skull on a Stick

A young boy runs across the grass rattling
a skull on a stick. The skull has a near
-perfect set of teeth, and it bursts out laughing
when it catches sight of them in the wing
mirror of a parked Ford Cortina. The more
the skull in the mirror laughs, the more the skull
on the stick laughs back, unaware it's laughing
at itself. *Are you my mother?* the skull
says to its reflection. Then the boy races
through the bishop's spacious and well-kept Palace
grounds. *Daddy!* the skull blurts after a swish
of purple vestments is ushered under guard
into the waiting mansion. Until the boy's mother
puts her head out an upstairs window, yelling:
Put that thing back where you found it this minute,
Martin, and get in here for your dinner.
The skull doesn't understand, but it smiles
widely with its near-perfect set of teeth.

Forget

Forget the Memorial Garden. It doesn't know
what it's supposed to remember. Could it be connected
to the name of the town: Tuaim = tumulus = burial ground?

Never mind. Was it for famine victims when it was a workhouse?
Or soldiers when it was a barracks? Or maybe the Mothers
and Babies when it was their Home? No.

What kind of home has high walls topped with broken glass?
Forget the Memorial Garden. It can't remember its secret
chambers, once used for sewage, remembers less the seven hundred

and ninety-six missing children. All that's on its mind today
is the thrush's nest in the Guelder Rose (which, by the way, knows
it isn't really a rose), and what haunts the garden most

are the blunt ends of the blue-green eggs. Will there be enough
air for the chicks to breathe before they break their shells?

Julia

*Julia Devaney, née Carter, spent almost forty years in the Tuam Mother
& Baby Home, and was one of those who locked its doors for the final
time on the 16th of September 1961.*

I. JULIA & THE ELDERBERRY TREE

It was the garden that saved her. She loved the garden.
Year after year she waited, patient as the elder,
letting every other tree come into leaf ahead of her.
And how modest she was, never trying to outshine

others in the shrubbery. Generous, too, and obedient,
never failing to offer blossoms bursting with nectar
in summer and branches heavy with berries
come September. Yes, her winter twigs smelled

unpleasant and her buds were ragged as hand-me-down
clothes, but the elder always felt alright as it was,
without mother or father. Like the elder, Julia
was hardy and light-loving. No regrets. No bitterness.

So, how wretched that it became known as the Devil's
Tree, the way those gathered at McCormack's
Corner would nudge each other when Julia passed,
whispering: *she's one of The Home Ones.*

II. JULIA CARTER & JOHN DEVANEY

Julia became the oldest ever resident of The Home.
Given up as a baby, nobody ever came to claim her.
It wasn't a prison. She had been free to leave any time
she pleased. A friend gave her ten shillings once
and she walked down as far as the bus station in Tuam,
but when two people from The Home came after her
she went back willingly. Where else could she go?

It was the garden that saved her. Being in the garden
wasn't as monstrous as being inside. She'd rather be
weeding than saying the rosary. In the garden
she never thought about not having a mother or father.
In the garden she felt no regrets, no bitterness.
One day, John Devaney saw her picking potatoes.
He looked at her the way the golden privet cupped

sunshine on the Dublin Road side in the evenings.
I'll take you away from this place, he said. *Marry me,*
Julia. My wife is three years dead and I've a fine
empty house all my own down Gilmartin Road.
She considered this, her head to one side, the way
a robin might an outstretched palm of breadcrumbs.
Arrey, what good am I to you out there? she said.

Sure, I don't even know how to buy a pint of milk.
John was an old man, Julia thought, but a good man.
And when she stepped into his house she felt

as if she had stepped straight into heaven. Her heart
expanded like a telescope. How small everything was.
His kettle the size of a teapot. His kitchen, cosy,
a perfect diamond-shape like the nest of a wren.

III. A HOLY SMELL

There are perfumes fresh as children's flesh,
soft as oboes, green as meadows,
and others, corrupt, rich, triumphant

    – Baudelaire

Nobody teaches a small child the meaning
of a smell the way they might encourage them
to recognize a colour, perhaps, or a word.

We teach ourselves smells and we are limited
by our experience. But it wasn't as if Julia
didn't know that particular smell well,

one of her chores to scrub the floorboards
after the toddlers had been made to sit for hours
on ceramic pots. Another to strip the 'mackintoshes'

from the beds in the dormitories each morning
and hang them to dry over the old iron staircase.
The stench was as familiar to her as the piggery.

No. This was a holy smell, sort of prayerful,
like light through stained glass or the whisperings
of a Hail Mary in an empty chapel.

What did Julia know about the exotic notes
of faraway olive groves? Or the supposed romance
of a palm tree? As far as she knew, all soap

was red and used to scrub skin, clothes and floors
alike. It smelled of the elder's winter twigs
and the night-time whimpers of unloved children.

Unbeknownst to Julia, another sort of soap
was used upstairs. Soothing green bars of Palmolive
promised *Freshness, Charm and Youth Prolonged.*

And without running water in The Home, the nuns
tipped their rinse water into their chamber pots
after washing themselves in the mornings.

It wasn't unreasonable, then, for Julia to assume,
when sent to empty them, that nuns had a God
-given gift for passing perfumed piss.

The Art of Keening

Once there were women who were paid to cry
when someone died, as if grief couldn't be
left to amateurs. When the keeners appeared
a whetted hush settled over the mourners.

Keening was a glorious release, a vocal
poultice that anointed every lesion,
every cleavage. To keen was to penetrate
grief the way darkness is pierced
by the sad arias of cows whose calves
have been taken away to be weaned.

Oh, how I bellowed involuntarily
as you were being born! Yet, when you died,
I'd quite forgotten how transcendent pain can sound
when it throbs inside a song's hollow vaults.

Clean

Dead is the happiest we ever were.
In life we were the hidden children
of sin. In death sweet gifts
of benediction for a congregation
of insects. How exquisite our decay.
You could say it was a washing
away of wrongs. Clean at last,
our commingled bones were rinsed
of flesh until a halo of moths foraged
softly on every last hair on our heads.

And now we are forget-me-nots, blinking
in the sudden sunshine of an autumn meadow
gone to seed, the cries of small children
catching on the slightest breeze.

III. THE SPECULATIONS
OF COUNTRY PEOPLE

Mar sin do fuaras agus má tá bréag ann ní mise do chum.

(That's the story for you, and if there's a lie in it, let it stand.)

The Speculations of Country People

*J'ai tendu des cordes de clocher à clocher; des guirlandes de fenêtre à
fenêtre; des chaînes d'or d'étoile à étoile, et je danse*

    – Arthur Rimbaud

Some say he isn't dead at all, that they've seen him dancing at night
in his human form on Trá Rábhach. He will never rest, like a steep
waterfall, or the devil, even though there are no saints left for him
to bring fish to, or bundles of firewood. The fact that he chuckles
during courtship endears him to me also. *Adorn yourselves, dance,
laugh – I'll never be able to throw Love out the window.*

*

*A hare paused amid the gorse and trembling bellflowers and said
its prayer to the rainbow through the spider's web.* Be wary as walk-
ing under a ladder, for a witch can take the form of a hare to steal
your milk and that of your neighbours. I have seen them suck all
the milk from a cow. And you will need plenty of milk, and can-
dles. Though a blemish to the face is a method of payment for less-
er offences.

*

On the island they say a master otter lives in the lake. So skilled
is he at fishing, he is noble enough to be hunted by kings. I hear
his screeches in the night and they make me wet when they be-
come more urgent. He is a beast of *fabulous elegance.* I unzip my
sleeping bag. *Magical flowers humming.* He pierces my neck and
carries me away. *Blood and milk flowed.* The rain becomes pliable,
arching its back to the wind that is coming, westerly, faster than
the earth can spin. He is so confident he lies down and goes to

sleep. Now I am on this sandbank in the dark. But look the other way, out to sea . . .

*

On the sand there is a grey seal. His song stops me and makes me blush. For all grey seals are really beautiful men who can charm a woman's heart, and heal it.

*

These are not the speculations of country people.

Brown

My childhood involved no frills or flourishes. It was sturdy, and down-to-earth, like the colour brown. When the low beam of memory shines on those years, my granddad is the prism that the light hits, that splits it into a rainbow of brown, from treacle to woodchip. Even the name of his birthplace sounds brown. *Togher*: safe passage through wetlands. The waters in Togher run brown from peat deposits, and his roots there went deep, back to his father's father. They were brown as the words of a place's history: as *famine, tuberculosis, eviction*.

The landscape of wood and earth drew Pop to it, like the colour of leaf litter embracing the mottled breast of a thrush. So many honest shades: the thick workman's weave of his trousers, the twill of his peaked cap, the oak of his three-legged milking stool. A farmer and a gardener, wherever he went, the earth he came from went with him, under fingernails and in the threads of his hob-nail boots. He carried the weather too, beaten onto his face and mottled into the backs of his hands. Brown as the words of a man who made a living from the earth: as *plough, rotovate, sow*.

Even the smells were smoke-brown. Turf fires in the small middle room, the mahogany of his pipe, inadvertently polished in his palm by years of ponderous handling, and the tobacco, either chewed and spat or pulled and blown into musky wisps. The shuffle of the cows in the dusky shed, and the unceremonious plop of steaming dung onto dry straw. And all my sun-filled summers, summarized in dead grass and molasses, fermented into the sweet perfume of silage.

The seasons cartwheeled along in a series of browns. Autumn was crayoned copper and bronze. It was harvest-brown, was the damp soil that clung to the sugar beet piled at the sides of the road; to the nuggets of potatoes the fields gave up into muddy hands; to the wild mushrooms, sprung overnight and welcome, come morning, as the outstretched arms of a just-woken toddler. It was bronze bales of hay piled up onto trailers to be stored in sheds with rusty galvanized roofs.

Winter was a brown mulch of autumn's leftovers, the sopping soil perfect for mud cakes and wellies' squelching. It was the skins of sheep turned inside-out and tanned to make my parents' thick his-and-her coats, to be added over blankets at night for winter burrows – myself and my brother beneath them, as snug as fox cubs. It was the naked branches of the beech, the horse chestnut, the ash, woven into child-sized forts.

Spring was the folding of the fields into furrows ready for planting, the plough rousing the landscape into a fresh brown patchwork of hazel, tawny and raw umber. It was me, busy with the business of being a tomboy, trying to disguise my chestnut ringlets under a cap and tramping the fields in my brown corduroy dungarees. Or offering my fingers to the soft muzzle of a calf so it might learn to suck milk from a dung-flecked bucket.

Summer was a millefeuille of brown because of the bog. Hours seemed to pass differently there. They got the slow polish of bog oak that you almost could reach out and stroke. In the bog, the sun and the wind worked in shifts to hug and kiss your skin until they had blended you into the sienna, taupe and walnut of their peat carpet. It was turf-brown like the hot tea in a flask a neighbour might bring you.

Can a sound be brown? The song of the skylark was, from a shrill hickory chirrup ascending right up until the tone was almost magnolia and out of earshot. The butt of my dad's shotgun was brown, and everything he tried to shoot with it wore the mute brown camouflage of not wanting to be caught. The kind of quiet I had to be, those times I trailed at his heels, was a brown shush like the wings of a moth.

No frills or flourishes. Rabbits hang from the rafters in the shed; a cock pheasant sniggers from the fairy fort behind the house my father built – and here's Pop, wheeling his High Nelly back the Toghermore avenue, the beech trees mighty all around him, a battered milk churn balanced on each handlebar. And there, somehow, am I, skipping along behind him.

Pop

i.m. Willie Joe Kelly, my Grandad, 1908–1988

An old man slaps a palm to the warm flanks
of his favourite cow – *easy now* – as she sways
up the path to be milked.

He leans his High Nelly against the whitewashed wall,
rotates the peak of his tweed cap to the nape of his neck
and crouches on a three-legged stool,
his forehead resting against the cow's belly.

He rolls, twists and squeezes – *easy now* – to coax the milk
from the soft, pink teats with all the finesse
of a pastry chef piping a profiterole.

Jets of almost yellow froth into a white enamel bucket.
Easy now – hooves shuffle over hay-strewn concrete,
and the swish of a tail conducts a troupe of contented moos.

A little girl's red wellies splunk in the sweet-wet muck
as golden flecks of hay twirl in a shaft of light from the gable.
Neither he nor she have ever heard of a profiterole.
Easy now . . . they let the cream rise.

Tomboy

Come, climb the tall scots pine in the churchyard
with me. We'll watch them go in to half eleven mass.
Just don't let Auntie Lil see you when she rings the bell.

Here, you can wear my Spiderman T-shirt; I like to climb
bare-chested, feel the twigs tangle in the ringlets
my mother makes me wear. I'll show you how to get

up onto the sacristy's flat roof, see how warm
the black tarred felt is under your thighs. Loll with me here for hours
against the pebble-dashery, until it's time to go top & tail

blackcurrants for Dolie O'Shea. We can play pitch & toss
against the old school wall with the coppers she gives us.
Dare you to crawl under the bridge into the big cement pipe

where The Glen trickles under Lizzy Murphy's boreen.
C'mon, I'll race you! Bet I taste like Moroney's penny sweets
in your mouth and that first fizz of 7up up your nose.

Feel the weight of this ingot wafer full of raspberry ripple
and Neapolitan ice-cream. I'll give you some if you come
inside my forest fort. I'll show you my green fern bed.

If only I could climb or crawl back far enough, I'd paint your
childhood's bloody knees with Mercurochrome, the deepest
antiseptic red. I'd tell you everything was going to be all right.

The Architecture of a Nest

i.m. Auntie Lil, my godmother
and my mother's godmother, 1926–2019

The long-tailed tit is a master of building nests.
Three weeks it takes her to finish each one:
back and forth to the hawthorn's fork,
embroidering moss with her needle-point beak

and tempering spider's silk with fine fox
-hair filigree, roofed with sea-foam-green
lichen, lined with two thousand feathers –
with her own, plucked out of her breast, if needs be.

Her little black head wears a tiny white crown.
Her long tail a tightrope balancing-pole,
her flock like teaspoons stirring the air,
she hangs upside down from the branches' ends.

My Auntie Lil knew the architecture
of a nest. An engineer of cosy, she would tuck you in
to a burrow of wool and cotton. O she was
my Walton's Mountain, my childhood's safest

of down-filled snuggery. I can still see her smile
when I'd call out, *Goodnight, Elizabeth!* –
the plastic of her pastel curlers, dimpling
under the criss-crossed brown of her hairnet.

Last Man on Omey

Based on 'No Stuntman is an Island', a 2010 Radio One documentary about the last permanent resident of Omey Island, Pascal Whelan, who died in 2017

When I was young here there was no start, no finish, no nothing. Everything was so natural. We'd catch crabs and race donkeys. We didn't know anything different.

People come back to be buried. My mother is buried here. She was Powell. Her people were shipwrecked here on their way to America from Wales, and they stayed. The first thing you come across is the graveyard. Funerals here are something to see. Some cars haven't left the church a mile away by the time the hearse has arrived. There'd be a line of cars across the sand from here to Claddaghduff.

Four or five cars are lost on the beach every year. I lost two in a week once, but that was just stupidity. One was a Ford. The front wheels were so light they floated. Everyone was having a good laugh over in Sweeney's. It's a complete island two hours before the tide comes in but I know when I can get out and when I can get back. It's not like a bus, the tide isn't going to be late. You have to plan your day around it.

I live out on the west side. This is the only road. It's about a mile long. Out there is Shark Island. That was moved off in the thirties I think, after a tragedy. That's High Island. There's a monastery there and beehive huts. Then Cruagh and, after that, America. The winter storms are fierce. It blew away once, my mobile home. Ended up three fields away.

I've no electricity but I don't really miss it. I've power enough for what I need from batteries. A kerosene lamp for reading. I'd like the running water though. I do miss that. I've a little eight-inch DVD player. That's me fencing with Peter O'Toole on the BBC. I taught him for a film he was in. None of it is rehearsed, by the way. Sometimes I miss the fancy hotels alright.

I used to be more self-sufficient, before I got the cancer. I liked to grow plenty of vegetables. Hopefully my energy levels will come back. On the windows I just grow tomatoes and spring onions. The garden is overgrown now. See, there's the bed of nails. The nails are all rusty, but feel how sharp they are. They're easy to make really. Just hammer away for a few days and there it is, your bed of nails.

This is the ancient well. Lots of people come over with a jar, for water, the water here is so good. And they leave little gifts at it, for their ancestors or whoever. There's an ancient church too. That's it in the hollow. It's slowly falling to pieces, but it's still there. There's another graveyard near the church. No headstones there, though, and the bones keep coming up out of the sand. Every time I pass, I bury some. Then I go to the well to cleanse myself.

This is a close-knit community. Well, I suppose you could say I'm close-knit because I'm the only one left. I'm not lonely though. People ask me if I'm lonely. I'd never be lonely. There's a difference between being on your own and being lonely.

A Retired Stuntman's Bed of Nails

He hammered away for a few days once and there it was:
his bed of nails. The nails are rusty now but still sharp.

Unfastening it from a blanket of grass he harnesses the bed
to his chest with a length of electric-blue fishing net and drags

himself and it across the sand at Trá Rabhach, past the Holy
Well and up through the sea thrift, and the wild mint on the cliffs

at Goreenatinny, saying the names of town-lands out loud
like prayers as he goes – Sturrakeen, Cartoorbeg, Claddaghduff.

The sea below is ruminant, chewing its bonemeal and dabberlocks:
this is a wild place, and the waves have many stomachs.

The wind here is a knife-thrower and the air thinly sliced.
Despite all this, he removes his clothes and lies down on the nails

in surrender, the way a lost anchor topples where it falls, arms
parallel to the sea bed. There he stays until his skin is all lobster

-orange and honest. He doesn't sleep. He just hums
as if he were the wings of a honey bee preparing for flight.

When at last she comes, he tells her: iron can only be happy
when it's rusty. He knows she won't stay. The sea knows too.

She doesn't have a high tolerance for salt. Nobody can live
permanently here. In the meantime, he does not want to escape.

Sea Thrift

It is getting colder and all my pink heads are dead.

Off with them! says the wind, my beautiful
executioner, its cries pushing out of the sky like knives.

West Cork Selkies

They haul themselves ashore, whiskered,
moonlit, and fin-footed, unzip their skins
and step out of them, effortless as from
the white fur coats they wore in utero.

By day they swim the bay as pinnipeds,
but every ninth night they walk the streets
of towns like Timoleague and Baltimore
as human beings with wide inter-tidal eyes.

Over pints of Murphy's and bags of cheese
and onion crisps, they discuss how many
more human husks they will have to discard
before they find what they are looking for.

Bladderwrack

O ancient sea-witch
from the kingdom
of Protista

stabilizer of ice-cream
and of a good head
on a pint of Guinness

I Think, Therefore I Am

not a nest made from earth feathers seaweed and all types of objects
       that float on the sea collected by male birds
not an ancient church in a hollow falling in on itself but still there
not the sea dropping human bones at the feet of the sand
       nice throwing sticks
not a little gift left at a holy well
not a sharp rock that cuts his hat through and penetrates his skull
       just over his right ear
not a city sitting solitary full of people
not Times Square when it was wolves and chestnut trees before the
       blight the odd mountain lion
not a cherry tree in winter a high priestess in her ordinary clothes
       not drawing attention to herself
not a foldable shopping bag an uneaten bag of salad a disposable
       coffee cup
not a gemologist a conglomerate a monarchy
not a bar-through-a-telephone-box concept or a secret reefer
       -smoking balcony for old hippies and jazzers
not a hotel's revolving rooftop that doesn't revolve just creaks right
       and left
not a clarinet taken from his pocket because he was also a musician
not the spray-painted word STOP
not the Tagalog word *gigil* the irresistible urge to pinch someone
       you love
not a language spoken over the entire world that will keep no more
       secrets from you
not a pint of Guinness a packet of cheese and onion crisps
not a Jesus nut that single point of failure
       with catastrophic consequences
       in a helicopter or the fruitcake in the crowd with the gospel sign

who do people say I am?
not a petrified animal penis
not a location for activities beyond the law like an island
    for naughty ladies

    because no man is an island
    all men are grey seals
    which are really beautiful men
    who can charm a woman's heart and heal it
    I think therefore I am
    bladderwrack
    multiplying its bladders
    in bad weather so it can keep its head
    above water which would explain
    my many grasping fronds
    my attachment to rocks

IV. LOVE, SIN, REPEAT

Blue

When I can't find a noun for what you are
to me, I think of how there was no word
for *blue* in Ancient Greek. Was it simply
beyond description or were they so exposed
to the colour they became desensitized to it?

Did they just identify what was useful
and disregard the rest? And are there other
colours we haven't found a name for yet?
Like when I first went to introduce you
and found I'd sailed beyond the wine-dark

horizon of my lexicon. (The word *boyfriend*
must have been set adrift somewhere
between middle-age and girlhood.) *This is my . . .
lover*, I said, but others got uncomfortable,
as if we'd taken all our clothes off.

What can I say? Not partner, not other
half. Not soulmate, not object of affection.
Not knight in shining armour, not Prince
Charming. Not my darling, my stud-muffin
Nor pumpkin, honey, sugar, sweetie-pie.

This is my cerulean, I'll say, my sapphire.
He's my cyan, my Aegean. You are midnight,
you are electric. You are sky and sea
to me and every other shade Homer had
no name for between violet and green.

Hymn

It's Sunday morning and you are moving
inside me like a song that begins
in the syrinx of a lark, invisible
to the eye, silky and golden
on the ear. No promises have I made
yet I thee worship with my body. I,
a sinner, unwelcome to receive the body
of Christ. I breathe you in as the curtains
of our church fall open on a Pink Lady
sky and the Owenriff river rushes past
the window, breathless and unrepentant
for its winter swell. My hymn hovers
– oh god oh god oh god – then rises again
to beat its milk-warm wings against the glass.

This Is Not a Proposal, but Maybe It Is

I.

I was never comfortable with The Word in my mouth. It was a
dropped crotchet, a missing beat, in the slow reel of what I thought
I always wanted. The first time I tried it to say it, The Word was the
July-rind of a crab-apple, drying and binding my tongue clumsy.
When The Word was in it, my mouth was an orb-spinning spider,
my tongue the still-inflated mating plug, The Word a tiny male,
who never suspected his heart would stop once she was impreg-
nated. And my mouth was a glass bottle, my tongue a stopper, The
Word a wasp in it. And my mouth a bay, my tongue a tide, swim-
ming against itself, breaking waves, The Word a rip current hidden
under it. And my mouth a cage for The Word, my tongue a heavy
thumb, The Word the wing of a cupped bird. And my mouth the
stretched skin of a goat on a bodhrán, my tongue a double-ended
knuckle bone trying to keep time. But even if The Word were laced
with isinglass, all the desiccated fish bladders in the world would
not have removed the cloudiness, made it any less astringent. In
the end, my mouth was a famine, my tongue the scar of an in-
complete road they made me build, criss-cross, up a mountain.
And it was obvious to everyone that The Word was going nowhere.
So I set fire to my tongue and kept my mouth shut.

II.

By the time I met you, my love,
my mouth was the bronze hollow
of a Brazen Bull. The Word cried out,
scattering its letters into a bull's bellow.

When the smoke cleared, my tongue
glinted with the bones of divorce
made into jewels, and I woke up
beside you, my mouth all hive, my tongue

frantic: *Soon there will be no more honey!*
it chanted. And it was dancing,
the dance of the bees, telling me how to get
to the sweetest nectar. I kiss your lips.

We glow honeycomb yellow. All of a
sudden my whole mouth is the forest
floor. My tongue stirs with petrichor.

It diffuses from the base of my throat.
The Word is a raindrop on a porous surface
after a dry spell. And I open my mouth, say it

over and over:
husband, husband, husband . . .

The River & the Lake

I am a river. You are a lake.
Me the Owenriff, you Lough Corrib.

Both bodies of water, we are not the same
(though our identities are interconnected).

When I sit, I am disciplined to fit
between my banks' chastising margins.

I fold my hands neatly, pin my legs
together and point stilettoed toes.

When you sit, you expand into all the available space, arms thrown
along rocky shores as along the back of a couch, legs
spread-eagled.

When I stand, I clench the currents
of my core, yank my shoulders back,

allow my chest to flow. When you stand,
you thrust your hands into your pockets

and lean against the pier at Oughterard.
I sashay downriver as if in pencil

-skirted hips. You watch me come
towards you, my river-mouth quivering.

The waves of your lake-chest heave,
mirror to the corrugated iron roofs

around us – how ripped you are!
How full of yourself! I love to feed you

constantly with fresh water
from the mountains of Connemara.

I am the kind of river that might like to bring
her man a single malt in bed and fluff

his pillows up so he can sip it
while she very gently rubs his balls.

Lichenology

*Lichen is an unnatural union between a captive algal damsel
and a tyrant fungal master*

    – Rev. James Crombie 1831–1906

Suppose a fox is sly, an owl
wise and a storm malevolent.
Then suppose lichen is a sensational
relationship between an algal
damsel and a tyrant fungal master.

Precisely how lichen is formed
is a mystery, but suppose
the fungus lured the algae to him
brimful of promise for a life
of bountiful moisture (the fungus

equivalent of rich, handsome
and a little bit audacious).
Suppose he is holding her
captive somehow, exploiting her
vulnerability so he can use her

unique tools for photosynthesis.
Suppose he made her read
all three volumes of *Fifty Shades
of Grey* in a weekend
and she liked it, in spite of herself.

And suppose she watches other
algal damsels going to work
on the bus or the train in Dublin,
London, New York or Paris
and asks what it is they are

reading behind the winter issue
of *Poetry Review* or *The Wall Street
Journal*, biting their lips
and insisting that the prose
is atrocious and there's nothing

in their lives that is missing.
Or suppose their symbiosis
is something other than conflict.
They seem at ease with each other.
Suppose they're onto something.

Suppose he didn't enslave her
and make her take his name,
that she cooperates willingly.
Suppose theirs is a clever survival
strategy, an equally beneficial

partnership with clearly defined roles.
Suppose she likes that he is bigger
physically so she can feel safe
in his embrace, the way he weaves
his filaments tightly about her

and sees to it that she gets the right
amount of light and water.
Suppose she goes about the making
of food gladly because when she's wet
she's turned on and it's then

they glow and grow as one.
Suppose lichen is happy.
Suppose happiness is a flourish of paris-
pistachio- and jungle-green
on the low branches of a willow

by the river after rain
the way there is nothing
more melancholy than bubble-gum
and hot-magenta cherry blossoms
on an April wind.

Emasculate

They were already dead when I took an axe to them, those true
bone extensions of his skull. He was in hard horn – a full, broad
palm on display, tines curved strongly upward, symmetrical as a
six-pack. Immense, and somewhat fascinating, they had become
cumbersome, superfluous structures hindering his progress
through the forest; over-burdened like a knight with too many
accoutrements – layers of leather and chain mail, heavy helmet,
steel plates, long-sword, scabbard and shield. My buck in velvet
was sensitive and protective, delicately turning his head sideways
between trees, and I was tired of picking up after him, snatches
of fabric snagged on saplings or strewn on the forest floor, though
one year I did fashion some into the most exquisite pair of shoes.

Destined to decorate a gatepost, to be a trophy, a museum piece or
a bridge over a rivulet, they were useless to him as a weapon,
their sharp points unexposed even with his head bowed right down
between his forelegs. To save him the gigantic effort of maturing
a new pair, I soldered the wound shut. And they didn't go to waste.
I up-cycled them. Antlers make wonderful buttons and necklaces.
It's such fun to embellish and polish them, like you would ivory.
My prize possession is a *Baton de Commandement* which fastens
dresses, straightens arrows and smoothes leather thongs. I even
sling spears with it. I really thought I was doing him a favour, until
last night, I dreamt an Irish Elk rise from a dawn-white mist
and those spacious ornaments looked so singular, and so beautiful.

Èit

Scottish / n. / aɪt / iyt. Placing quartz stones/crystals in streams (e.g., so that they shine/sparkle in the moonlight, thereby attracting salmon). Lomas lexicography, 2017

Let me take away your pain, the river says, to the silt and pebble
    in its depths,
caressing them. I can hear this, though its mouth is far away. I
    want it to care
for me too, not least because it knows exactly where it's going –
and when it moves, it moves like an inviolable oath. Somehow,
    this tells me
it always keeps its promises. I can tell this also by the intensity of
    its eye contact.
It looks at me the way the midday sun gets under its skin,
like a searchlight looking for pike under rocks, right down into
    those places
where shadows flatten themselves, their ears pinned back as
    though someone
spoke of them. There should be a word for the strong desire to
    follow
a river, I am thinking, as I lean from the boat and put my lips to
    its skin,
in the Catholic tradition of kissing blessèd things. This is how to
    find out
something personal about the soft rush of an otter, the homeward
    thrust
of a trout. But mostly, about the stroke of an oar. It's no
    coincidence, then,
that when I trail my hand in the water, it feels as if I am running
    my fingers

through a lover's hair. I wear a life jacket, at first. But this is a
    precautionary
measure. It's just me and the river, learning to trust each other. At
    last,
when it invites me into its bed, I start to sparkle, the way quartz
    crystals do
when dropped into the water to attract salmon in the moonlight.
The trembling of the river above me is like that feeling you get in
    the pit
of your stomach when you are with somebody that you love. *But
    you don't
love me,* I say to the river. *What is love anyway?* the river says, yet so
unconditionally that it sets me gently rocking, the way you did
    that day
in the hammock by the river. Which reminds me of how I was told
not to rock the baby too much or I would spoil it. Spoil it? Why is it
knocked out of us nowadays, that deep longing to be rocked?
The Owenriff was clearly rocked plenty as a young river. For
    which I will be
for ever grateful to the wild-about arms of the mountains of
    Connemara.

Inadvertent Love Poem to Your Ex-Wife

He must have known, much as a trout can smell
a single drop of home in a million gallons
of seawater, because he finally stopped crying
as soon as you arrived at the hospital
in your ex-wife's country, and held him to your chest.

This is where I am safest, he was saying.
Dad will be the one to make my school lunches
and remind me to brush my teeth. He'll be the one
to drive me to discos and tease me about girls
I might have kissed. Dad will teach me how to fish.

So when your house phone had cried out that morning
above the urgent huffing and puffing
of the river you could see from the window
of your sitting room, it was as if the Owenriff knew too,
as if it had come to full term after all that fleshy

December rain. You watched its waters break
without warning all over your lawn. And as you tell me
the story I try hard not to wish that *I* was the river
at the part where you admit: its body was never
more beautiful than when it swelled that winter.

Mon Petit Futur Gourmet

The Golden Goat Hotel balances four posh hooves
on the crest of a rock over the Côte d'Azur. He can even
point out Bono's house below near the ochre shore.

This hircine vista placed the pearl of a song
on my boy's tongue every morning for a fortnight
when he was six. He'd throw back early morning

curtains, his little mollusc mouth wide open to serenade
the blue and green horizon – *Oh the Med, Oh the Med,*
Oh the Mediterranean Sea! – as if it didn't know its own name.

Shunning the *Menu Enfant* for a plate of naked vegetables
he'd spend five minutes marvelling over a pea tendril
snaked around his finger as if he were David Attenborough

in a rainforest handling an anaconda; or rearranging
an edible canvas of nasturtium, viola and calendula petals
like Van Gogh considering a field of sunflowers.

Futur gourmet, the waiter called him, and not the fussy
eater they whispered about at children's birthday parties
when he refused cake, fizzy drinks and chips.

Today I watched his twelve-year-old self deliberate lemon
juice versus tabasco on an oyster, and savour peppery rocket
and pungent pecorino on a pink forkful of beef carpaccio.

Do you remember La Chèvre d'Or? he'll often ask, curling
each 'r' handsomely à la française. I think then
he is polishing that pearl, awaiting, patiently, his return.

Florence, Easter 2015

*I wish that we might laugh at the remarkable stupidity of the
common herd*

> – Galileo Galilei

I am sitting between the warm terracotta braids
of a Florentine rooftop with my fourteen-year-old son.
We are planning where we are going to go tomorrow.
A full moon is rising at the other side of the river
above Museo Galileo, and we find ourselves humming
the Declan O'Rourke song *Galileo* as we hug our knees.
The dusky cupola of the Duomo nipples the skyline,
and lanterns Lungarno glow crème-anglaise yellow.
Vespas purr up at us intermittently from the cobbles
along with the smell of garlic and espresso.
Over at the Ponte Vecchio, an infantry of selfie-sticks
periscope the streets like curious meerkats.
We wonder if they have read that selfie-taking
killed more people last year than sharks, and laugh.
Then Ethan says: *Nobody knows what the last words
on the moon were, you know*. Eugene Cernan said: *Ok.
Now let's get off. Forget the camera.* Then: { . . .} static.
The last part was heard by the crew of Apollo 17
alone. It's a mystery between brackets. I am telling
you things, poem, that I wouldn't tell Facebook.

The Homeless Woman Who Thought She Was a Goose

A grey goose wanders into a posh grocery shop on Exchequer Street
to peck at a ciabatta, the guttural *rhut-rhut-rhut*
of her feeding chuckle audible to all the other shoppers.

Ordinarily partial to the whiff of game, they scrunch-up their noses
at the stench of her unkempt feathers, skewer her
with dirty looks and make for the exit. The nice girl at the checkout

apologizes for the inconvenience and the manager erects a notice:
Feeding waterfowl is harmful. It interferes with their survival instinct.
It discourages them from eating insects, larvae, and small molluscs.

In the refrigerated section, the goose opens a jar of goose fat
to rub some up and down each winglet and across her décolleté,
as if she weren't goose enough. Intending to make a down

payment, she assembles a stainless steel trivet at the cash register
and anchors her skin with one wing, so she can give herself
a rough, dry pluck with the other until she has exposed

the layer of gossamer under her regular feathers.
Her neck skin is loose and tears easily. She signals a shop assistant
to work his fingers under the slit, right down as far as her thighs,

snipping any difficult fibres and sinews with a kitchen scissors.
Then asks him to massage her criss-crossed scores
with olive oil while she pierces herself lightly all over with a fork.

Her breasts will be edible ever-so-slightly pink and there are plenty
who would sample them, for *he who eats goose*
of Michaelmas Day, shan't money lack or debts to pay.

When she slips from the Quays into the cold arms
of the river that evening, the glow of streetlights bastes her goose
    flesh
and her bluish wishbone tightens, foreboding a bitter winter.

Lowering her head as she swims under each bridge of the Liffey,
regardless of its height, she bows goodbye to the city; behind her,
    a skein
of ever-decreasing Vs point around the bend and out of sight.

Michaelmas Daisies

The fishing has finished. It is the beginning
of hunting season. It is the time to pick apples
and the time to make cider.

A lost flock of Sebastopol geese
shuffle from a pond on Stephen's Green.
They do not know that it is Michaelmas.

Their eyes are ocean blue, their down
a flounce of soft white curls, matted
under filthy blankets and damp cardboard.

The streets are impractical
for their gaudy orange slippers. When handled
carefully, they are chatty and gregarious

but, when ruffled, can be haughty and raucous.
Some gorge on blackberry cider,
sickly-sweet as if the devil himself had pissed in it.

Others place stones on their tongues
to muffle their honking, so they can peck
undetected in the bins outside McDonald's.

More settle in Georgian doorways,
beak under wing, with scribbled petitions
hung from their gizzards.

These geese now bedizen the city, perennially,
like the blue and purple hues of Michaelmas daisies
that grow in wayside places, with no care at all.

Come Sing the Song of the Dead

The children of our sins are dead. Forbidden to grieve, we take refuge in the trees so that we might keen in peace. At first, no sound at all will come. We are dumb as we were on the birthing table when they made us swallow our pain, fists in our mouths. But grief isn't burrow-loving. It doesn't take readily to cages. Grief is a wild thing, the queen of all venery. It won't be domesticated. To sob quietly into our pillows was to tease grief with delicacies it used to eat in the wild like tender twigs and ripe berries. The meat of grief, being dark and strong-smelling, is liable to leap off in all directions and often doubles back on itself. Sometimes it will wait, watching you until you're almost on it – and then one bound, long and high, and it's out of sight. Where does it go for weeks on end? It's in the woods. Deep in a place of ochre upon ochre, russet under russet: a place like that, where muffled light through branches tests our silence, and the leaves give way to bees. The sound is low to begin with, like the humming of wings preparing for flight, but rises quickly, as grief does – as, finally, grief comes home to us. We wear the sound now like a shroud. Tomorrow, we'll emerge from hiding. We will process through the town, our dead children on our shoulders, rattling their skulls on sticks and singing the song of the dead for everyone to hear.

ACKNOWLEDGEMENTS

p. vii. *What it takes, on this planet* . . . : Pablo Neruda, 'Poor Fellows', from *Five Decades: A Selection (Poems 1925–1970)*, ed. and trans. Ben Belitt (New York: Grove Press, 1974), p. 179.

p. vii. *Shame requires the eyes* . . . : Anne Carson, 'Shame Stack', *London Review of Books* 34:8 (26 April 2012).

p. 37. *There are perfumes fresh as children's flesh* . . . : Charles Baudelaire, from 'Correspondances', *Les Fleurs du Mal* (Paris: Poulet-Malassis et de Broise, 1857). Translated by Majella Kelly.

p. 43. 'The Speculations of Country People' incorporates or adapts quotations from Arthur Rimbaud, *Illuminations*, trans. John Ashbery (New York: W. W. Norton, 2011), as follows:

J'ai tendu des cordes . . . : From the poem 'Fragments du feuillet', p. 64.

Adorn yourselves, dance, laugh . . . : From the poem 'Phrases', p. 61.

A hare paused amid the gorse . . . : From the poem 'After the Flood', p. 19.

beast of fabulous elegance . . . *Magical flowers humming*: See the poem 'Childhood', p. 27.

Blood and milk flowed: From the poem 'After the Flood', p. 19.

p. 67. *a romance of lichenology* . . . : Reverend James M. Crombie, from 'On the Lichen-Gonidia Question', *Popular Science Review*, vol. 13, July 1874.

p. 71. *Scottish / n. / ait / iyt. Placing quartz stones* . . . : Tim Lomas, from 'The Positive Lexicography Project', https://hifisamurai.github. io/lexicography/.

p. 75. *I wish that we might laugh* . . . : Galileo Galilei, from a letter to Johannes Kepler, August 1610, as quoted in Stillman Drake, *Galileo at Work: His Scientific Biography* (Chicago: University of Chicago Press, 1978), p. 162.

To the judges who placed these poems (or versions of them) in competitions, thank you. 'Virginia Creeper' won the Strokestown International Poetry Prize 2019. 'Voice' won the Ambit Annual Poetry Competition 2018. 'Portrait of the City with Mastectomy' came second in the Gregory O'Donoghue International Poetry Prize 2018 and was published in *Southword*. 'Sonnet for the Glass Blower' came third in the Resurgence Eco Poetry Prize 2016 (now called the *Ginkgo Prize*). 'Emasculate' was runner-up in the Dromineer Poetry Competition 2016.

To the editors who first published these poems (or versions of them), thank you. 'Lichenology' and 'Funeral' in the *Irish Times*, shortlisted for a Hennessy Literary Award. 'Blue' in the *Irish Times*. 'Michaelmas Daisies' in *Poetry Ireland Review*. 'The Art of Keening' in *The Well Review*. 'Bosch's Garden of Earthly Delights' in *Rialto*. 'Sex' in *Cyphers*. 'Tomboy' in *Quarryman*, literary journal of University College Cork. 'Mon Petit Futur Gourmet' in *Skylight 47*. 'Clipping a Cockatiel's Wings (For Dummies)' online in *The Pickled Body*, in the *How to Make Love in Dangerous Times* issue, and subsequently in the *Aesthetica Creative Writing Annual*. 'Cortège to Omey Island as Umbilical Cord' was a Poetry School pocket poem for Poetry Day.

Thanks to Mam and Dad for just about everything, but especially for being there to support me as I tried to raise a child as a single parent. I couldn't have done it without them. Or without my brother, Larry, and his partner Olivia. Special thanks to Larry for all the delicious food and wine along the way.

Thanks to my son, Ethan, for being my most forthright critic and my most ardent fan, all rolled into one. And for his unique way of seeing the world, which is a constant inspiration.

Thanks, Frank, for the love and the laughter, and the unique gift of living by the Owenriff. Big thanks also to your sons, Eamonn, Joey and Tom, for accepting me so graciously into your home.

Thanks to Catríona Courtney and Bernie Healy, my besties from my UCC days, for over three decades of friendship. And to two of the finest Cork men I know, Michael Morris and Mark Long, my brothers from other mothers, the three of us born in the same forty-eight hours.

To my Tuam Bridies: Lola, Tomasa, Sandra, Irene and Caroline. For that thing that makes a Bridie a Bridie. Ye are wide for it. Thanks for that.

Thanks to Sarah Byrne and Gabriella Attems, my poet sisters. I am grateful to poetry for bringing us together ten years ago. My life and my writing have been all the better for it.

A huge thank you to the wonderful writing family I gained on the MSt at Oxford, during which time many of these poems were written. Special thanks to poet and senior tutor Jane Draycott, and to my classmates and friends Gry Strømme and Millie Guille.

Thanks to Claire Cox and Niall Munro, and all at the fabulous Ignition Press, for publishing a selection of these poems in my debut pamphlet, *Hush*.

Thanks to the University of Leeds and the sponsors and organizers behind the Brotherton Prize, especially Stella Butler and John Whale. Thanks also to the other members of the judging panel: Vahni (Anthony Ezekiel) Capildeo, Malika Booker, Melvyn Bragg and Simon Armitage. And to Carcanet for publishing ten of these poems in an anthology of the prize.

I am grateful for the support of my colleagues in St Colman's, Clare-morris, especially to Jimmy Finn, whose steady hand at the helm I greatly appreciated. Kudos to my colleague and friend Rory Hynes, who decided we should sign up for creative writing classes after work in 2013. Be good professional development, he said. Look how that turned out!

To all the fine young Mayo men that have filed in and out of my class-room for over half of my life now. It's the *Howya, Miss* and the *Thanks, Miss* that have gotten me through each working day. So, thank you back. Special thanks to my LCA lads. Watching you all find a path-way through education that nurtured you, at last, has been the most rewarding part of the job.

Shout out to poets Susan Millar DuMars and Kevin Higgins. Susan's creative writing class in the GMIT was the one that Rory and I signed up for back in the day, and it was where I wrote my first poem. I went on to take some of Kevin's classes and to read in the Galway library at one of their *Over the Edge* events. They do so much to support emerging and established writers in Galway and beyond.

Thanks to the Poetry School. I have taken many of their online courses. Its tutors and community of poets have been a tremendous help to my creative practice. And to the poets who I have been lucky enough to be a student of and to be inspired by over the years, the likes of Jo Shapcott, Helen Mort, Maurice Riordan, Billy Collins, Leanne O'Sullivan, Caroline Bird, Mimi Khalvati, Daljit Nagra, Johnathan Edwards, Colette Bryce, Samantha Wynne Rhydderch and Sinead Morrissey, to name but a few.

Thanks to Padraig Stevens, for generally encouraging me to write, and specifically for placing a recording of Julia Devaney's voice into my hands, knowing full well that poems would follow.